Kids' Poems

Teaching Third & Fourth Graders
to Love Writing Poetry

Regie Routman

SCHOLASTIC

NEW YORK • TORONTO • LONDON • AUCKLAND • SYDNEY
MEXICO CITY • NEW DELHI • HONG KONG

For Elizabeth

Acknowledgments

A special thanks to all the wonderful students and teachers in the Shaker Heights, Ohio, City School District who helped make this book possible. In particular, I am grateful to teachers Maria Baker, Jennie Nader, Norris Ross, Lee Sattelmeyer, Linda Schlein and Nancy Schubert, who welcomed me into their classrooms and collaborated in teaching poetry writing. Heartfelt thanks also go to Jennie Nader and Lee Sattelmeyer for their thoughtful responses to the entire manuscript.

I am most appreciative of my insightful editor and friend, Wendy Murray, who has the heart and soul of a poet. Wendy embraced this project with great enthusiasm and sensitivity and followed through on every aspect with great care, respect, and attention to detail. Thanks, too, to Terry Cooper for her enthusiastic endorsement and to Kathy Massaro for her bold, innovative design. Finally, thanks to my husband Frank who lovingly supported the entire project.

Cover and interior design by Kathy Massaro
Cover illustration by Laura H. Beith
Back cover photograph by Kalman & Pabst photo group
ISBN: 0-590-22735-1

Contents

The Kids' Poems

* POEMS BY THIRD GRADERS

Summary of Instructional Plan for Poetry Writing in Grades 3 and 4

Before you begin

✳ Read poetry aloud
✳ Establish a poetry corner
✳ Consider poetry notebooks
✳ Examine anthologies
✳ Ask students, "What do we know about poetry?"

Suggested Sequence of Instruction for First Lesson

✳ Sharing kids' poems
  ● Examples of what we notice and discuss
✳ Writing the first poems
  ● Affirming writers' efforts
  ● Capturing the "gems"
✳ Sharing and celebrating

Ongoing, Self-Perpetuating Loop of Instructional Follow-up Sessions (minilessons)

✳ Demonstrating: Supporting Budding Poets
  ● Sharing, noticing, and discussing more kids' poems
  ● Teacher modeling
      Thinking aloud and writing in front of students
  ● Trying out new kinds of poems
      Writing in the style of another poet
      Writing small poems
      Writing poems across the curriculum
✳ Writing poems independently—total free choice or expected experimentation with a new form
  ● Affirming writers' efforts
  ● Capturing gems
✳ Sharing and celebrating

Publishing the Poetry

✳ Creating an anthology

Why Free-Verse Poetry Writing?

Teaching poetry writing is my favorite teaching. It's fun, it's exhilarating, it's easy. Every child is successful and writes with care and energy. So how do all students come to write well and enjoy the poetry-writing process? Reading and discussing poems by kids just like them hooks reluctant writers and all writers into believing that poetry writing is doable and pleasurable.

And while third and fourth graders have typically had some experience with poetry writing, often that experience has been limited to poems that rhyme. Because creating poems that rhyme is hard for most children, kids wind up spending most of their time searching for rhymes—whether they make sense or not—and often their poems end up sounding contrived.

The experience is quite different with free-verse, nonrhyming poetry. Here kids shine. Released from the structure of rhyme, kids can focus on content and language, and they express themselves easily. After seeing, hearing and discussing many kids' poems, children feel confident to write on their own. As they do, they have fun with language, space, and form. They play around with words and images. They create their own rhythms and patterns. Their voice— each child's unique and personal style—emerges.

Kids who don't like to write—for a whole host of reasons—write free-verse poetry with ease. They love that their poems can be short, about anything at all, and arranged to the writer's specifications and whims, and that they require little revision. They love the freedom. Strict rules that apply to other writing genres can be relaxed with poetry. Every year there are students who "take off" with poetry writing. Bennie was one such student. A reluctant third grade writer who struggled with academics, he experienced immediate success and pleasure writing poems. The affirmation he received boosted his confidence and willingness to write. See his poem, "School," next page.

I first started teaching poetry writing to students several years ago when I realized that writing in most classrooms was pretty limited—mostly journals, reports, assignments, and other traditional school forms. If there was poetry

School

School is a learning place
You can do different things
Like computer
Reading
Writing
Social Studies
and learning about the states too
School is a learning place.

—By Bennie Marshall

writing, it was usually the rhymed version or a structured, rule-bound form like haiku. When I looked at the writing I do in my life, it was quite different—mostly letters, notes, cards, faxes, and, yes, poetry. I write free-verse poems for myself and for others as one way to express my thoughts and feelings, and I love doing so.

"Why not teach this to students?" I thought. I began doing just that. Beginning with students in kindergarten, I have continued to be amazed and delighted by the wonderful results. All kids blossom through poetry writing. So do teachers. You and your students will experience this same success, pleasure, and affirmation.

Fourth grade teacher Nancy Schubert concurs:

It frees students from the restrictions I grew up with in poetry. I do a lot with haiku and cinquains, but I had never done free verse before, mainly because I didn't know how. Poetry is a place where all children can feel success. All the kids enjoy it, the boys as much as the girls. Poetry writing forces kids to pay close attention to language. They're all very serious about it. They all do well.

About This Book

Kids' Poems will show you and your students how to write free-verse poems quickly, easily, and successfully, using peers' poetry as models. The message I want you to take away from this book is: *You can do this too*. Initially, it will require a leap of faith to trust the poems themselves and your own judgment to know how and what to teach. It can feel risky to try to teach something where there are no scripted lessons and where kids are given a lot of freedom. But the process is easy and structured (see page 4), planning is minimal, and the payoff is huge. My hope is to guide you comfortably through the process and give you confidence to begin teaching free-verse poetry writing in your own classroom.

Specifically, *Kids' Poems: Teaching Third & Fourth Graders to Love Poetry Writing* will show you how to:

* get started with writing poetry

* use kids' poems by students of similar ages (included in the second half of this volume) to inspire and teach poetry writing

* write a poem yourself as one model to share with students

* inspire students to write about topics that have personal significance

* share and celebrate children's efforts

* write in the style of another poet

* write small poems

* write poetry in the content areas

* teach elements of poetry, such as imagery, line breaks (where each line of the poem ends on the page) and white space (space on the page with no words), ending lines, topics, titles, and choosing language carefully

* create a poetry anthology

Getting Ready to Teach Poetry Writing

Poetry needs to be heard and experienced! Before you start writing poetry with your students, you will want to spend at least several days—or better yet, weeks—immersing them in this genre. Read poems aloud, create a poetry section in your classroom library, examine poetry anthologies (commercial and student), find out what students know about poetry, and give students lots of opportunities to read poetry—independently, with partners, and in small groups.

Rather than relegating poetry writing to a one-time "unit," make it a vital, ongoing component of your curriculum. While any time of year works well for teaching poetry writing, I like to begin early in the school year. All students have early writing success which, in turn, transfers to other writing. As well, students choose to read and write in this genre all year long, at school and at home.

Read Poetry Aloud

Read your favorite poems aloud to your class. Begin to notice what poets do, but don't dissect the poems. Enjoy them! Our own love of poetry is contagious. I recommend reading only free-verse poems because this is what students will be writing. While students love rhyming poems, they will find these on their own. Let kids know that most of the poems in the world are nonrhyming poems— free-verse poems where the writer determines the form and pattern.

Establish a Poetry Corner

Keep an area just for poetry all year long. Bring in your favorite poetry books, and encourage students to do the same. Sign out anthologies from your school and public libraries. Be sure to have lots of books of free-verse poetry, and select some that are related to topics of study in your curriculum (see pages 30–34 for writing poetry in the content areas). The richer your collection is, the more models for your students. Eventually, you will also have anthologies by your own students, and these will serve as the most influential models of all.

Consider Poetry Notebooks

Some teachers have students keep poetry notebooks, not just for the poems students write but also for copying favorite poems to read and enjoy. Having the language of favorite poems close at hand makes it easy to go back to memorable wording, to enjoy rereading poems, and to be influenced by particular wording when writing. Some students also enjoy memorizing and reciting favorite poems.

Recording captivating language is exactly what I do when I read. I have a separate notebook where I copy beautiful, memorable language that I don't want to forget and that I can refer to and read again. I always list the page, book, and author when I copy the quote. This allows me to find the original source and give proper attribution when necessary. We need to teach our students that if they use an author's words, the author needs to be credited.

Examine Anthologies

Leaf through several poetry anthologies while holding them up for students to see, and ask them what an anthology is. (Once I have student anthologies, I include these too.) With prompting and guidance, students determine that a poetry anthology is a collection of poems by various poets.

Let students know that they will be creating a classroom anthology with one or more poems from each student. Give them at least several days to look through the anthologies you've gathered. (Sustained silent reading time works well for exploring these.) Let students know that you and they will be deciding together exactly how the anthology will look, be organized, and be completed (see page 35).

What Do We Know About Poetry?

Before you begin teaching poetry writing, find out what kids think about poetry. Their attitudes and perceptions can guide your teaching.

In Maria Baker's fourth grade class, I brainstorm with students and write using the overhead projector so all can see the responses and so that we have a record to return to (see next page).

What We Don't Like About Writing Poetry

✺ It's frustrating because of having to find rhyming words.

✺ It's really hard.

✺ It's frustrating figuring out what the poetry should be about and what to call it.

✺ I don't like poetry writing.

What We Do Like About Writing Poetry

✺ When it's actually done, it sounds good.

✺ I like saying rhyming words.

✺ It's my idea.

✺ It takes up my time when I'm bored.

✺ You can make it any style you want—funny, serious, sad, scary.

✺ I like to read it. I get ideas from the books I read.

✺ Sometimes a poem is very descriptive.

✺ My poetry relates to what's happening in my life.

✺ It's fun to read when it has lots of voice.

—Mrs. Baker's grade 4 class, January 1998

Maria's students' responses to poetry are typical. Some kids like it, some don't, but just about all believe poems have to rhyme. After such an exercise, I say something like the following to students:

You are all in for a treat. I am so excited! We're going to learn to write poems that are fun and easy to do. But we're not going to write rhyming poems because these are very hard for most people to do. We're going to start by looking at poems other students just like you have written. I can't wait to show you these poems and enjoy them together!

Once students have had some experience with writing poetry, I often revisit our initial chart. In a shared writing, we add to the chart and notice how our perceptions have altered and our knowledge about poetry has grown.

Beginning to Teach Poetry Writing

You might want to begin the first poetry-writing session with "What do we know about poetry?" or you may choose to begin by sharing and discussing kids' poems. Sharing kids' poems sends the immediate and powerful message: "Kids just like you wrote these poems. You can do it too." Seeing poems in kids' original handwriting, on a variety of topics, dispels any notions about writing being hard, long, or requiring strict conventions.

Framework for the First Lesson

The first lesson begins with a sharing of kids' poems, moves to independent writing supported by brief conferencing, and ends with a sharing session:

✳ **sharing kids' poems** (15 to 20 minutes)
✳ **sustained writing** (25 to 30 minutes)
✳ **sharing and celebrating** (10 to 15 minutes)

Sharing Kids' Poems

My goal in focusing first on kids' poems is for students to see that a poem can be about anything, is easy to create, reveals something about the writer, and has a unique form and shape.

I read aloud and show at least five or six kids' poems. I begin by saying something like the following:

Wait until you see the poems I'm going to show you, poems written by other students just like you. These are nonrhyming poems, what we call free verse.

They're easier to write than rhyming poems. I want you to carefully listen to and look at these poems as we enjoy them. See what you like. See what you notice.

Until you have your own collection of poems, start with the ones in this book.* These poems are written by students just like yours—students who excel in school and students who struggle, students who like to write and students who avoid writing. These are first draft poems, thoughtfully conceived and swiftly written with minimal revision. (You will notice some circled words on some drafts; this occurred later, when students were checking spelling while editing the poem for publication.)

It is the kids' poems by peers that, most of all, provide the models that spur budding poets into confident action. As you develop a collection of kids' poems to use from year to year (remember to save original drafts and final copies, with kids' permission), you will find that students delight in recognizing the poems of older siblings and siblings' buddies.

Making Poems Visible

Because I want students to see the poems clearly, I put them on overhead transparencies. (Feel free to make overheads of your favorites—both the drafts and final copies—in this book.) While you could also gather your class closely together and read aloud the poems and show them to students, being able to easily zero in on individual words and features—and perhaps use an overhead projector pen to point out particulars—makes projected transparencies my first choice.

Discussing the Poem as a Whole

Once again, because I want to instill a love of and ease with poetry writing, we primarily enjoy and discuss each poem as a whole. I have learned from experience that kids easily take in all the elements at once—the title, topic, line breaks (where the line ends on the page) and white space (space on the page without print), imagery, rhythm, ending line, and more—so we discuss all of these as we talk about the poem. Rather than overwhelming students, talking about the poem as a whole seems to help them internalize the essence of poetry. In succeeding weeks, we work on the separate elements as necessary (see pages 19–29).

Keep in mind that there is no formula, no right or wrong way, to read and discuss kids' poems. The poem itself will guide you as to what to address.

---

* At the beginning of third grade you may want to refer to my book *Kids' Poems: Teaching Second Graders to Love Writing Poetry*.

Examples of What We Notice and Discuss

I usually read each poem aloud twice. Before the first reading I say, "Listen to so-and-so's poem about such and such." I read the poem without commenting and show the student's handwritten draft. Showing the draft affirms that a peer "just like you" wrote the poem. For the second reading, I say, "Listen and look carefully as I read this poem again. What do you notice that the writer has done?" Now I show the final copy as I read it aloud so that students can easily follow along and read the poem to themselves.

Here are a few examples of how it goes.

Regie : [after second reading of poem "Bad Days," page 76] I bet you can really relate to this poem because everyone has bad days. I like the way the writer tells exactly what went wrong. Look closely at how she sets her poem up on the page. She writes in sentences but she lays it out so it looks like a poem. That's part of the fun of writing a poem. You can make it look whatever way you want. With a poem, you create white space. That's the place on the page where there's no writing. You get to decide. What else do you notice?

Paula: I like how she ends it.

Regie: Read those lines for us.

Paula: "Oh, I should have stayed in bed, I said."

Regie: Yes, notice how this is very different from the way you might end a journal entry. The tone changes. You can tell the poem is over. Anything else you notice?

Everett: I like her title.

Regie: Yes, I like it a lot too. Titles are important. Notice her title, "Bad Days," sets us up for what's coming in the poem.

I read "Football!" by Taylor (page 80). I want kids to hear and see that a poem can be short and still say a lot.

Regie: I love this poem. Taylor writes about something important to him—he tells us what it is by his title, "Football!", and he expresses himself honestly in just five lines. I've experienced what he is feeling, and I feel sympathetic. Probably you did too. Listen and look carefully as I read it again. What do you notice?

Ryan: He's upset. He says, "Taylor can't catch!" He puts himself in it.

Regie: Yes, and notice how he does that.

Sam: He uses quotation marks.

Regie: Yes, because that's what someone else has said about him. What else does he do?

Davis:	He says he can catch if he's not under pressure.
Regie:	Right. Lots of us do better when we're not under pressure. Notice how Taylor makes "when I'm not under pressure" his last line. I think that's a powerful ending. He ends with what he most wants us to know about him. I'm going to read the poem one more time. Listen to how my voice stops briefly at the end of each line, where the line breaks on the page. When you write your poem, keep rereading it as you go along to be sure it sounds and looks exactly the way you want. Look again at the decision Taylor made when he set up his poem on the page. Notice his white space, places with no words.

* * *

Regie:	Let's take a look at Casey's poem, "Thanksgiving" (see page 42). As I read it the first time, listen to how Casey uses all her senses to create a memorable picture of this holiday [reads poem while showing draft on overhead projector]. Okay, now I'm going to read it again [reads from final copy]. What do you notice?

Kara:	I like how she starts a lot of her lines with "I smell, I see."
Regie:	Yes, I like that a lot. Let's look [points to phrases while reading them]. "I smell…, I see…, I see… I smell…, I see…" She creates a pattern, doesn't she? By repeating these phrases she gives the poem a lovely rhythm. Poets often use repetition to create an effect that strikes us when we hear and see the poem.
Nate:	I like how she describes each thing.
Regie:	Like what? Give us examples.
Nate:	She doesn't just say "macaroni." She says "cheesy macaroni boiling."
Regie:	Yes, exactly. Poets choose their words carefully, just as Casey does. I love how she says, "I smell the crunchy stuffing with little juicy bits of turkey." That brought back a picture for me of cooking my own Thanksgiving turkey each year. What else? What about her ending?
Tabitha:	She says "breathtaking surrounding." I was picturing a beautifully set table with lots of relatives around.
Regie:	Good for you. She doesn't say that, but it's certainly implied. I also like how you can tell her poem is over. She changes the rhythm a bit for the last lines. That gave me a sense of closure. When you write your poem, think about how you want the ending to look and sound.
	Look at her draft again. See all those lines she put in? Those are line breaks— lines that show where Casey decided that each line of her poem would end. You can put those line breaks in later, but it's often easier if you just think about those line breaks while you're writing.

Continue along in a similar manner with several more kids' poems. You'll find that the discussion happens very naturally and easily by listening to and looking at the poems. Even if you have never done this before, you will be successful. (For more examples of noticing specific poems, see pages 23–29.)

Writing the First Poems

Once we have seen, heard, and discussed a bunch of kids' poems, we move into 25 to 30 minutes of quiet writing time. I say something like the following before students begin to write:

You have just seen and heard a bunch of poems by students just like you— poems about feelings, family, pets, school, friendship. We've also been listening to and reading lots of poems these past few weeks. So you know that a poem can be about anything at all. And, as you saw, you can set it up on the page as you like. Your poem can be long or short, serious or humorous. Choose your words carefully. Reread as you go along to be sure your poem looks and sounds exactly the way you want it to.

If you finish early, start another poem. Put your name on each poem. Skip lines as you write so you have room for changes if you want to make them. Afterwards, you may choose to share your poems. Have fun writing!

Typically, almost everyone gets to work and easily chooses a writing topic. Based on all the models they have seen, students easily grasp that poems are often about things that produce a strong feeling.

The quality of even the first poems (many are in this volume) is always a delightful surprise. Every time I have worked in a classroom with poetry writing, there is at least one "reluctant" writer who shines and—with his very first poem—produces his best writing work to date. Taylor (see "Football!" on page 80) was one such student; Bennie (page 6), was another. School was hard for these boys, and they didn't like writing or feel successful as writers. But poetry seemed to have special appeal. I have repeatedly observed that it's not just the content that improves with such writers; when kids care about their writing, they willingly put more effort into their handwriting and spelling as well.

Affirming Writers' Efforts

As students begin to write, I walk about the room to briefly confer with each student, kneeling down so I am at their eye level. My main purpose here is to encourage and support writers' efforts. Sometimes, if a student is having difficulty choosing a topic, I may need to have a brief one-on-one conference.

The following comments are typical ones that I make as I meet with students. Usually, I make one such comment and move on.

✳ I like that title. I know exactly what your poem will be about.

✳ I saw you rereading your first few lines. That's what thoughtful writers do.

✳ I see you crossed out here to make your poem sound more interesting. That tells me you're thinking carefully about how your poem sounds.

✳ You seem to be having trouble getting started. Let's think together about the poems we looked at today. I know you have [a pet] too. You could write about that. I'll help you think about how to begin.

✳ I like the way your poem looks on the page and how you've skipped lines to make stanzas (lines grouped together; see page 29).

✳ I love the way those words sound together. You're choosing words carefully.

✳ Great job. I can picture exactly how you were feeling.

Capturing and Celebrating the Writing "Gems"

As I make the rounds while students are writing, I am on the lookout for writing "gems"—words and phrases that are especially well crafted. Then, I stop and draw everyone's attention to what the writer has done well. For example, I will say something like: "Everyone, stop for just a moment. I want you to hear how James begins his poem. I love the rhythm." Or, "I've asked Shauna to read her poem. Listen to how intricately she describes her brother."

Noticing the gems serves several purposes. It:

✳ reinforces something the writer has done well and encourages him to continue

✳ shows the class what a good poem looks like and sounds like

✳ gives students ideas for their own writing

✳ sets expectations for quality

Later, once students are on their way, writing with confidence, I do not interrupt writing time. I wait until sharing time to notice and celebrate gems. But for the first session—and perhaps the second—I want students to be immediately affirmed. Sharing the gems also promptly establishes peers as writing models, a powerful influence. The sharing of gems goes very quickly.

Some Examples

Regie: Danielle, read your title and first four lines.

Danielle: "My Sister Kayla, Silly, Crazy, Abnormal, Strange."

Regie: I like how you use powerful adjectives and put each on a line by itself.

(See completed poem, page 68.)

Regie: Anna, read what you've written so far. Listen to the mood Anna evokes and her unusual topic.

Anna: [reads title and what she's written so far, first seven lines].

(See completed poem, "Shadows," page 86.)

Regie: Tim, just read us the title of your poem.

Tim: "Baseball Stress."

Regie: Great title. I can tell—without reading any lines—that you are really going to put yourself into this poem and describe how you feel.

(See completed poem, page 82.)

Sharing and Celebrating

After writing time, students who are eager to share do so. Sometimes we gather in a whole-class area. Other times students stand up at their writing place and read their poems. And often students will share with partners or in small groups. Because our main purpose in poetry writing is to free kids up to write, to make poetry writing fun and easy, and to give all kids confidence in their abilities as writers, we do not use sharing time to critique. Sharing time is primarily for congratulating writer's efforts. Occasionally, as students recognize the superior quality of a poem, they break into spontaneous applause. At times, I will quickly point out something that the writer has done especially well. But mostly, we just listen to and appreciate each writer's efforts. Sharing time goes fast. Because poems are seldom more than a page, everyone who chooses to share can do so.

Follow-up Sessions

The first session has gotten us going. Everyone has successfully started or completed one poem, and poetry writing continues as a teaching focus. That is, for several weeks—and for at least three days in a row each week—writing demonstrations take place followed by sustained time for students to write poems independently and to share them. During our poetry-writing focus, students are expected to complete at least three poems—more if possible—and to try their hand at using a different form and style after it has been modeled and discussed (see pages 22–34). It is important that budding poets continue to have lots of demonstrations for writing poems.

The Format of Poetry-Writing Sessions

While subsequent poetry-writing sessions follow the same basic format of the first lesson, the demonstration that always begins each session may vary. That is, in addition to sharing and discussing kids' poems (and focusing on particular elements of those poems) as a demonstration, the teacher may write a poem and show her thinking-composing process.

Poetry writing follows the structure and procedures of writing workshop. The whole-class session includes:

- **demonstration** (5 to 15 minutes) one or both of the following:
  - **discussing kids' poems—includes minilessons woven in on aspects/elements of poetry**
  - **teacher thinking aloud and writing a poem**
- **sustained writing time and conferencing** (20 to 30 minutes)
- **sharing and celebrating** (10 to 15 minutes)

Time allotments will depend on your purposes and the needs and interests of your students. (While all aspects of writing workshop, including conferencing and editing, are integral to poetry writing, they are not discussed in detail in this book. For a full description, see my book, *Conversations: Strategies for Teaching, Learning, and Evaluating*, published by Heinemann, 2000.)

Demonstrating Before Each Writing Session

Ongoing demonstrations are necessary to ensure that students have ideas for writing, expectations for quality, an understanding of the elements of poetry so they apply them to their own work, and the knowledge and confidence to write independently. Many of these demonstration lessons arise in response to what kids are already doing or attempting to do.

Demonstrating with More Kids' Poems: Sharing, Noticing, Discussing

At the start of a writing session, share several kids' poems (from this volume or from your own students, with their permission) and ask students what they notice. As outlined on pages 11–14, while you enjoy the poem, talk about such features as:

- choosing a topic
- using just the right word to say what you mean
- selecting precise verbs
- deciding on a title

- writing with voice (unique, personal style)
- including conversation in a poem
- experimenting with line breaks and white space
- crafting the ending line

Teacher Modeling

Our own writing—and our willingness to share it—are very powerful models for our students. Even if you are uncomfortable thinking aloud and writing in front of your students, try writing a poem as they write so that at least they see you in the act of writing.

If you have never written in front of your students, take the risk. It will pay big dividends. Going through the process ourselves also sensitizes us to what we are asking students to do. (See example of one teacher's risk-taking, on page 24.)

Thinking Aloud and Writing in Front of Students

For our second poetry-writing session in Lee Sattelemeyer's third grade class, my demonstration begins with sharing several kids' poems and then moves on to my writing a poem.

When I am writing in front of students, I try to keep my poems on a level comparable to what most students are able to do. I choose a topic that resonates for me and that may have possible connections for their own writing. Other than considering what I might write about, I do no preplanning. I want to remain authentic in my demonstration; that is, if I am asking students to write "on the spot," I need to do the same. Such demonstration writing also has the advantage of not creating extra "take-home" work for teachers.

Here's how I think aloud in front of them:

> *When I was thinking about what I wanted to write today, I couldn't get Juliette out of my mind. She's a very dear friend to my husband Frank and me, and her eighty-sixth birthday is next week. So I'm going to write about her.*

Regie: [standing next to the overhead projector with a blank transparency and overhead marking pen in hand] I think I'll just call it "Juliette" [writes it]. You know, Juliette is old but she doesn't seem old. I admire her so much. I think I'll begin, *When I am old, I want to be like Juliette* [writes it on two lines]. Let's see:

> *Give parties* [says words while writing them]
> *To people I love*
> *Cook wonderful food*
> *Wear zany clothes*
> *Wear high heels*

Can you believe she still wears high heels? She has a pair of bright red ones that I just love.

> *Read great books* [continues to say words while writing them]
> *Walk everywhere*

Regie: Okay, this is a start. I'm going to read it from the beginning and see how it looks and sounds [while reading, adds *interesting* to third line, "give parties"]. I'm going to cross this out [strikes *To people I love*] because it breaks the rhythm of a list I seem to have going here. [Keeps reading, crosses out *wear* and inserts and says] *Buy.* [Continues reading and speaks aloud while writing.]

> *When I am old*
> *I want to be like Juliette.*

Regie: I think I want to end it the same way I started it, but this poem isn't quite right yet. I'm going to work on it some more because it's important to me. Then I'll show the poem to you again.

See the beginning draft below and the completed poem which I gave to Juliette for her birthday. See also Kelly's poem, "Claudia," (page 72). Notice how my poem has sparked a tribute to her mom.

Juliette

When I am old
I want to be like Juliette
Give ~~interesting~~ parties
~~To people I love~~
Cook wonderful food
~~wear~~ zany clothes
Wear high heels
Read great books
Walk everywhere

When I am old
I want to be like Juliette

For Juliette

When I am old
I want to be like Juliette

Love deeply
Have young friends
Dress elegantly
Wear high heels
Create beauty
Write books
Entertain beautifully
Picnic in the garden
Buy wonderful gifts
Stand by my principles
Share my emotions
Talk about art and politics
Read great literature
Garden every day
Give elaborate parties
Cook wonderful food
Savor meals with friends
Drink good wine
Walk everywhere
Celebrate life

When I am old
I want to be like Juliette

See next page for two other poems I composed while thinking aloud in front of students. One is a serious topic, worrying about my aunt's illness, while the other is a fond memory of my grandmother.

Trying Out New Kinds of Poems

I expect all students to try writing different kinds of poems. That is, in addition to having writing days where students have total choice on topics and form—mostly inspired by the kids' poems they have seen—on other days students are expected to write a particular kind of poem. For example, I expect students to try their hand at writing in the style of another poet, writing small poems, and writing poetry in the content areas. Use follow-up sessions, such as those described on the following pages, to specifically demonstrate alternate ways to write free verse and to give students time and opportunities to try out and practice various forms of poems.

Writing in the Style of Another Poet: A Sample Demonstration

One book that has been particularly helpful for opening up possibilities for writing topics and style has been *Baseball, Snakes, and Summer Squash: Poems About Growing Up* by Donald Graves (Boyds Mills Press, 1996). In free verse, Graves writes about what it was like when he was a kid. He captures memorable experiences such as his first girlfriend, hating certain vegetables, his dog, giggling in church, being teased, and much more.

For our demonstration in one follow-up session, I read aloud several of Graves' poems and ask students, "What do you notice?" Through shared writing, we slowly compose a chart of what Graves does as a poet. Later I word-process our list and give each student a copy to keep in their poetry folder.

For this session—and sometimes an additional session—I expect everyone to try writing in the style of Graves and to refer to our list to be sure they are on track. But first it is important I demonstrate by writing a poem myself.

Regie: You know, Graves's poem, "Faking It," about when he got sick because he didn't want to do his homework, reminded me of something similar that happened to me when I was in school. I would get so nervous for a test that I would pretend to be sick. I didn't do it often, and I was such a good student that the teacher and my mother always believed me. I think I'll write about that. I'm going to put conversation into it and tell how I felt.

I stand next to the overhead projector and write straight down the page as I speak out loud. As I always do while I write, I reread every few lines as I go along to be sure it looks and sounds the way I want it to. (See my poem, right.)

Afterwards I tell students:

> *Today I want you to write in the style of Donald Graves. Refer to the guidelines we wrote together. Be sure you write about something important to you, try to use conversation, tell your feelings, and put yourself into the poem. Have fun writing.*

Faking It

"We'll have the social studies test right after lunch," my teacher says.

"Oh, no," I think.
"I don't get that stuff."

Before I know it
I have the teacher by my desk.
"Mrs. Carver. I have a
    terrible headache.
I have to see the nurse."

"Ok, dear. Go right on down."

She doesn't suspect
She believes me.

I feel awful
I'm a truthful person
But I'm scared
Of failing the test.

At home I think
That was the last time
I'll pretend to be sick.

I keep my promise
until
"We'll have the science test
    at the end of the morning..."

A Teacher's Influence on Students' Poems

In one similar demonstration, I am working with Jennie Nader's fourth grade class. Jennie has never written a free-verse poem before, let alone in front of her students. I strongly encourage her to try. As Jennie's students begin to write, she does too, sitting quietly off to the side but with her students in view. Not only does her poem serve as a writing model; her willingness to risk, and to write about an embarrassing moment that many kids can relate to, sends the message that poetry can be used to write about difficult moments. Her writing spurred several of her students to write about difficult times. "Baseball Stress," on page 82, is one example.

I Don't Want to be Last!

We're going to be playing kickball.
We have to pick teams.

Yeah! cry the boys and girls
Oh, no! I say to myself.
Will I be picked?

Jeanette, Kurt, Chuck,…
I wait!

Missy, Chris, Dan,…
I wait!

Will anyone pick me?

We're down to four students.
I don't want to be last!

Michelle, Julie, Jim,…
Two more left.
Will someone pick me?

The captain twists her face.
Begrudgingly she calls the next name.
I look down.
And silently wait.

She shouts across the field
I'll take…

My name is called.
I breathe a sigh of relief.
Finally picked.
And not last.

by Jennie Nader

Demonstration Focus: Small Poems

Kids love writing small poems. Small poems demand less for some students and are fun to write for all. Such poems are also challenging because every word is important and makes a statement. Until I had kids' poems, I always began my demonstration by reading, noticing, and discussing poems from *all the small poems and fourteen more* by Valerie Worth, illustrated by Natalie Babbitt (Farrar, Straus and Giroux, 1996). These are mostly poems about ordinary objects, closely observed, with such topics as porches, a pig, coins, a caterpillar, and pebbles.

As with all poems I use as models, I read a bunch of these and ask the students, "What do you notice?" Some things we notice and discuss together are the layout and shape of the poems, the economy of words, the metaphors and similes, the descriptive language. For our session today, I expect everyone to try a small poem. Notice wonderful first attempts by Samantha and Greg.

Marbles

Soft and shiny
fits
in your hand
Glassy
colorful
like a small stone
You roll,
Over and over.

—Samantha Miller

Guitar

I remember in 1st grade at the end of the day,
my teacher always played the guitar,
letting us choose what she should play.

I remember right before she put it away,
everybody got to pluck a string.

And now that I play the guitar,
I remember being influenced by all those sounds,
ringing out to me.

I remember…

—By Greg Thiel

Read, examine, and enjoy the small poems in this volume with your students: "Fence," "My Pencil," "Instruments." Use these, along with Worth's, to inspire your own students.

Minilessons

Examples of minilessons are delineated on the following pages only to illustrate possibilities for poetry writing and discussion using the poems in this book. Remember to let the poem itself guide you in determining how and what craft focus to incorporate as part of demonstrating before each poetry-writing session. Keep your focus on enjoying the poem and on instilling possibilities and confidence to your young writers.

Selecting Topics

Notice with your students what kids have written about. Some topics and poems are humorous and clever, as in "Mix-Up" and "Honey Do's!" Others are pensive and serious such as "Storm" and "Shadows." Others reveal true feelings about difficult situations, as in "Divorce" and "Finally My 'Dad' Came 'Home.'" Many topics are about everyday life: best friends, as in "My Best Friend" and "Richard,"and family as in the poems about siblings and pets. Use the table of contents to examine what third and fourth graders typically address.

Writing With Voice

Let students know that poets write with voice—a unique style that shows the writer's personality. When a poem has strong voice, you can often tell who the poet is, even without the writer's name on it. One way to encourage students to write with voice is to tell them, "Write as if you are talking or writing to a friend."

A few examples:

* "My Sister Kayla" by Danielle Jones, page 68. Danielle's specific, illustrative language not only gives us a vivid picture of her sister but also a clear understanding of her love, ambivalence, and strong emotion.

* "Stepbrothers" by Taronna Bradford, page 60. To express her true feelings about a new family addition, Taronna moves from matter-of-factly finding out about having stepbrothers to her last line, "Uh. Oh. More trouble."

* "Tomboy" by Marnie Zoldessy, below. Marnie clearly and confidently expresses the different ways her family views her and how she sees herself:

Tomboy

Everybody says I'm a
tomboy,
even my family.
My sister tells me I need
to be more girlish.
That's not me.
My mom makes me wear dresses.
That's not me.
But my dad says,
"Come on, let's play ball."
That's my dad
who knows
me.

—By Marnie Zoldessy

Choosing Language Carefully

Careful use of words can create images, moods, and depth in a poem. Here are several more examples to spark observation and discussion.

☀ "Fence" by Benjamin Oakley, page 38. Note how Benjamin masterfully uses economy of words to create a vivid picture of an old fence.

☀ "Dream" by Katie Stamm, page 74. Katie writes emotionally of missing her Grandpa, who recently died. She repeatedly weaves in "dream" and "dreaming" to mark her painful loss and remember good times.

☀ "Honey Do's!" by Ryan Carris, page 50. Discuss Ryan's humorous and clever word play with "honey do's" to express exactly how he feels.

☀ "Shadows" by Anna Hutt, page 86. Talk about how Anna creates a scary mood and tone through repeating "shadows," often followed by strong verbs such as "creeping," "watching," "staring," "chasing." Note how her descriptions of where the shadows are, such as, "in the dusty dresser drawers" and "behind the rocking chair that creaks when it rocks," deliberately create an ominous tone which captures the poet's fright.

☀ "I Hear" by Gabriel Mack, page 46. He uses lyrical language to write a beautiful, "quiet" poem. He invented "people commotioning" and we left it alone because it sounded so right for the poem.

Notice Gabriel's draft on page 46. He is a bright student who struggles with writing and spelling. It would be so easy to view his poem only from the standpoint of poor mechanics and overlook him as the talented writer he is. Over and over again, I have observed struggling writers like Gabriel release their language facility through poetry.

Using Line Breaks and White Space

Line breaks help to set the rhythm of the poem as well as to create the white space and shape of the poem. As you look through kids' poems with your students, notice the many different ways students have arranged their poems.

For example, discuss with students how in writing "My Sister Kayla" (see page 68), Danielle has carefully considered line breaks and white space. Notice how she has multiple stanzas (a stanza is an arrangement of a certain number of lines). Danielle uses stanzas of three or four lines each interspersed with phrases such as "who loves," "who needs," and "who gives"—all of which are thoughtfully spaced and arranged to give the poem a unique shape and rhythm. And in "My Pencil" (on page 40), observe how cleverly Alex arranges his words on the page to correspond with his message of his pencil growing smaller.

Encourage students to have fun experimenting with line breaks and white space as they shape their own poems. Kids easily grasp the notion of line breaks and white space because they have heard, seen, noticed, and discussed many poems together before attempting to write on their own. Notice that the majority of poems in this book have been drafted with line breaks and white space without specific directions to do so.

However, when a student or students have written without line breaks, I teach them how to think about and apply the line breaks. Most often, I'll say something like:

> *Think about how you want your poem to sound and look. I'm going to read your first line. Do you want it to sound this way or that way? Should we end it here or here? Which way sounds better to you? Put your line break there.*

With the student's permission, I'll put her poem without line breaks on an overhead transparency. I'll read the first lines several times, each time pausing in a logical but different place so that the student hears and sees the different possibilities. Then I'll ask where I should place the line break(s), and I'll read it again to be sure that it sounds good to the student. Once the student seems comfortable, I'll stop and let her take over on her own.

While I model line breaks all along and we talk about them while discussing kids' poems, I don't emphasize them until kids are editing. And even then, I continually remind kids that they can set up their lines however they wish.

Poems Across the Curriculum

When fourth grade teacher Nancy Schubert and I experiment with writing poetry across the curriculum, we are delighted by how successful and enthusiastic students are about this writing venture. Nancy and I have been working together using small, student-led conversation groups to discuss the Southwest (part of our required social studies curriculum on regions of the U.S.) and the desert (part of our required science curriculum on biomes), and it has made sense in terms of time and content to combine the two related units. Through reading and discussing trade books, first-hand accounts, the district-adopted social studies text, and poetry books, we gather lots of information. Then, we use poetry writing as one way for students to show what they have learned.

Nancy and I begin our poetry-writing session by listening to, noticing, and discussing several poems that we select from *Cactus Poems* by Frank Asch, illustrated by Ted Levin (Gulliver Books, 1998); *This Big Sky* by Pat Mora, illustrated by Steve Jenkins (Scholastic, 1998); and *Storm on the Desert* by Carolyn Lesser, illustrated by Ted Rand (Harcourt Brace, 1997). I read each poem twice. Then I ask, "What did you notice?" Our shared writing, originally handwritten, is reproduced below exactly as we brainstormed it.

What We Notice

- using the same words at the beginning of each stanza
- all about the same topic
- can be written in the first person
- pattern changes at end
- a lot of description
- alliteration (several adjacent words that begin with the same sound)
- first and last lines may repeat
- metaphors used in many (comparisons without like or as)
- mood, tone
- humor
- may pose questions
- white space
- words go with the shape

Next we brainstorm topics of study that students might choose to write about. Our list, which reflects what students had read about, discussed, and previously studied, is shown on the next page.

Southwest Topics

- night in the desert
- being a cowboy
- animals (such as snakes, mountain lions)
- corn
- living in a Southwestern town
- birds
- visiting a ghost town
- mining
- water
- desert
- Colorado River
- Grand Canyon
- mesas
- cactus
- Hoover Dam
- Anasazi
- adaptation
- plants
- horseback riding

Brainstorming Words and Phrases Before Writing

Before I expect students to write, we choose a topic as a class—cactus—and then we brainstorm words and phrases for possible use in a poem. I write these words on an overhead transparency (see right).

- Next, referring to our cactus list and writing on a projected transparency, I begin to compose a poem and think aloud in front of students. I say and write, *What am I?* (See draft and completed poem on page 32.) After observing my composing process, students are instructed to choose one of our southwest topics,

prickly
holds water
long roots
long life
makes lots of homes
home for all for many animals
flowers
tapping to get water
like a faucet
hands or branches
huge
grows slow
thick stem
good defense
can take heat
dry
hot
ancient
amazing plant
rubbery green
expand and contract
lives in desert
useful after death
gives shade
used for food for Indians
always useful

brainstorm their own possible words and phrases for their topic, and attempt a poem. While I give students the option of using our list and writing a cactus poem, interestingly, no student goes that route. They all choose a topic that particularly interests them.

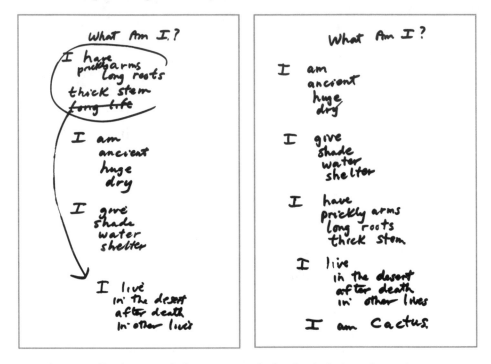

Once I have walked around the room and checked that each student is engaged with a topic, I continue my poem and complete it. Nancy also attempts a poem and begins writing it on the chalkboard so that students can see her composing process. I continue to write my poem on a projected transparency, so students can easily see it when I share it with them.

Some Examples of Poems by Students

Several students, influenced by the poems they have heard and seen and by my modeling in writing "What Am I?" choose to write in the first person. (See "Colorado River," page 84.) See, also, "Mountain Lions" (page 33). Use poems by notable writers as well as kids' poems, once your students write them, to demonstrate possibilities for writing poems across the curriculum. Use your librarian to help you locate outstanding poetry books that connect with your curriculum study.

Deserts
What Am I?

Dry and hot
as far as you can see
Birds   flying over me
Canyons   deep below me
cactuses   growing,
rivers   rushing
animals   trampling.
Storm comes
rush toward the
arroyo.
I am hard and
solid.

—By Anne Jiao

Mountain Lions

Smart creatures
hiding in mountains
waiting for something to eat
Something comes.
The other animal fighting for its life.
It's over.
The mountain lion has won the battle
Stays put for another animal to attack.

—By Jeff Harris

Who Am I?

I scream in everyone's ear
I rush over every rock
I fall at every waterfall
I shape every turn
I flatten every boulder
I give water to every animal
Who am I?
I am the Colorado River.

—By Tian-Tian Jin

A Summary of Poetry Writing in the Content Areas: What We Do

- Choose a curriculum focus (social studies, science).
- Immerse students in related poems; bring in books and read poems.
- Read and reread poems (What do you notice? Brainstorm list).
- Brainstorm possible topics for poems.
- Brainstorm words and phrases that go with one topic/title.
- Demonstrate how brainstorming can become a poem.
- Refer back to list of what we noticed about poems we read (teacher model with student support).
- Have each student choose a topic from list of possible topics and attempt a poem.
- Require quantity, at least 3 to 5 poems. (Optional: you could require at least several pieces of content-related information in a poem.)
- Choose a favorite or best poem to bring to publication.

Of using poetry writing at the end of an in-depth, social studies unit, Nancy Schubert says:

It plays into students' interests about the topic. We combined our study of the Southwest with our desert biome focus in science. We used trade books, first-hand accounts, the social studies text, and poetry to get information. We took notes and discussed in literature conversation groups. Everyone was successful.

Publishing

Almost all students word-process or handwrite at least one favorite poem after getting it into final form. I usually expect students to write several poems and then choose one for publication. During poetry-writing time, once students have revised their chosen poem and edited it (perhaps with a peer), I have a final conference with each student. Since the poems are rarely more than a page long—and often less—these conferences go quickly. Also, because students have chosen their poem's format, the usual burden for exactness in capitalization and punctuation—although these remain important—is eased somewhat, causing all students to invest seriously in the editing process.

Creating an Anthology

Kids love having a classroom anthology to call their own and show off their hard work. After examining anthologies, brainstorm possibilities for what your anthology will include. The anthology you and the students create can be as simple or complex as you decide. Some teachers have each student bring one poem to final edited form, usually with an accompanying illustration. These are bound simply into a classroom book, and each student gets a photocopy to read and keep.

Other classes go to elaborate lengths to produce a beautiful anthology, and many include an "about the poet" page (from the teacher, too) to go along with each poem. I have found that students can do most of the organization of the anthology with guidance from the teacher. See chart (above) from a shared writing for the final decisions made by one class. Notice that students volunteered for particular jobs, including designing the front and back covers and end pages. One fourth grader, Samantha Miller, was so inspired by poetry writing that she published her own beautiful anthology (see next page).

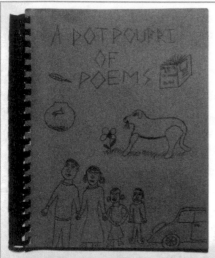

CONTENTS

The cover, a table of contents page, and a poem from a fourth grade anthology, "A Potpourri of Poems."

Buck Teeth

Hi, I'm Justin and I hate
being called buck tooth.
All my friends call me buck tooth,
beaver, rabbit.
I hate those names.

Justin Fort

Cover and one page from Samantha Miller's anthology.

Showtime

Song and dance
That's what the actors do
The wonderful sounds of Judy Garland
The clever moves of Gene Kelly
I watch them
I dance
I sing
I pose

Closing Thoughts

ree-verse poetry writing will inspire, encourage, and delight your students. Best of all, everyone will be successful. Your students, like all the students I have worked with, will experience ease and joy in writing in school, perhaps for the first time in their lives. My hope is that you and your students will learn to love writing poetry.

I leave the final words to Edward and Eileen.

Poems
Poems can be funny, sad angry or mischievos
I like poems, because you can
express
your feelings freely
without
worring about people
laghing at you
I like poems

Poems

Poems can be funny, sad, angry or mischievous
I like poems, because you can
express
your feelings freely
without
worrying about people
laughing at you
I like poems.

—By Eileen M. Kanost

Poetry

Paeceful
soft nice voice
Poetry

Poetry

Peaceful
soft nice voice
Poetry

—By Edward Allen

Fence

old
worn down
dried out
hallow

The old fence
sittes
in the yard

torn down
now this fence
is just a
pile of wood.

—BY BENJAMIN OAKLEY

Fence

old
worn down
dried out
hollow

the old fence
sits
in the yard

torn down
now this fence
is just a
pile of wood

—Benjamin Oakley

MY Pencil

My pencil starts big
then I sharpen
it gets smaller
smaller

smaller

smaller

gone

—BY ALEX STOUT

My Pencil

My pencil starts big
Then I sharpen
it gets smaller

smaller

smaller

smaller

gone.

—ALEX STOUT

Thanksgiving

I smelll the/chezey mocorony/
bding/I see the/turky/in the oven
steeming/I see the/slippery/cramberry/
souses/ on the table/I smell the/
crunchy/ stuffing/with little jucey,
bits of/turkey/I see the/big
fat/delicous/turkey/in a/breth,
taking/ sorounding/

—BY CASEY BASS

Thanksgiving

I smell the
cheesy macaroni
boiling.
I see the
turkey
in the oven steaming.
I see the
slippery
cranberry sauces
on the table.
I smell the
crunchy
stuffing
with little juicy bits of
turkey.
I see the
big fat
delicious
turkey
in a
breathtaking
surrounding.

—CASEY BASS

Instruments

Soft or
Loud
Nice and
Clear
just like
a bird
chirping
in the
air.

—BY GREG THIEL

Instruments

Soft or
Loud
Nice and
Clear
Just like
A bird
Chirping
In the
Air.

—GREG THIEL

I hir

the wind

blowing and

peppel ckomoshowing

Leavs swishing

somtims I

hir nothing but
sielints

—BY GABRIEL MACK

I Hear

I hear
the wind
blowing and
people commotioning

leaves swishing
sometimes I
hear nothing but
silence

— GABRIEL MACK

Mix - up

Sometimes my mom mixes me up.
Do this.
Don't do that.
That mixes me up.

Sometimes my dad mixes me up.
Wash the dishes.
Help me.
Come here.
Never mind.
That always mixes me up.

Sometimes my sister mixes me up.
Wash my gym cloths.
Don't wash my gym.
That mixes me up.

Some my friends mixes me up.
You can use them.
You can't use them.
That really mixes me up.

Sometimes my grandma mixes me up.
Give me this
Give me that
That mixes me up.

I all mixed up.

— BY ANDREA MARTIN

Mix-Up

Sometimes my mom mixes me up.
"Do this."
"Don't do that."
That mixes me up.

Sometimes my dad mixes me up.
"Wash the dishes."
"Help me."
"Come here."
"Never mind."
That always mixes me up.

Sometimes my sister mixes me up.
"Wash my gym clothes."
"Don't wash my gym clothes."
That mixes me up.

Sometimes my friends mix me up.
"You can use them."
"You can't use them."
That really mixes me up.

Sometimes my grandma mixes me up.
"Give me this."
"Give me that."
That mixes me up.

I'm all mixed up.

—ANDREA MARTIN

"huny dos"!

*Evry day when I come
home my mom alwase ses,
Huny do this, huny do that.
Huny do the floors huny
do the stars, I hate huny
dos, I hat huny dos.
          huny dos
          huny dos
          huny dos.

—BY RYAN CARRIS

"Honey Do's!"

Every day when I come home
My mom always says,
Honey do this,
Honey do that
Honey do the floors,
Honey do the stairs,
I hate honey do's.
I hate honey do's.
   honey do's
      honey do's
         honey do's.

—RYAN CARRIS

SCRUFFY

~~He~~ going to get a dog
~~He~~ was at the pound
~~He~~ Named him Scruffy
Scruffy went home with us

~~He~~ Wags his tail a lot
Picky eater
Barks at everything
Runs away
Proud of his home
I love him

Scruffy

—BY NATE ROBBINS

Scruffy

Going to get a dog
He was at the pound
Named him Scruffy.
Scruffy went home with us.

Wags his tail a lot
Picky eater
Barks at everything
Runs away
Proud of his home.
I love him.

Scruffy

—NATE ROBBINS

53

If you had a cat named Furball

If you have a cat named Furball he's nothing but trouble. He'll nock over the garbage can and blame it on the dog. He'll hang out with the bad alley cats and prowl the streets at night. He'll use the washing machine instead of kitty litter to do something disgusting. Huh what do you say? Oh. That's my cat.

— BY DANIELLE JONES

If You Had a Cat Named Furball

If you have a cat named Furball, he's nothing but trouble. He'll knock over the garbage can and blame it on the dog. He'll hang out with the bad alley cats and prowl the streets at night. He'll use the washing machine instead of kitty litter to do something disgusting. Huh? What do you say? Oh. That's my cat.

—DANIELLE JONES

Divorce

My parents got divorced
I don't like it at all
nope
I don't like it at all
But it sticks in my head
Like it's stuck to glue
Like it's stuck to glue
But one day
I'm gonna pry off that glue
And get rid of it
Forever
I don't know where
I'll put it
I guess It'll just stick
In my head
like glue

—BY SAM WINEGARDNER

56

Divorce

My parents got divorced,
I don't like it at all.
Nope,
I don't like it at all.
But it sticks in my head
Like it's stuck to glue
Like it's stuck to glue.
But one day
I'm gonna pry off that glue
And get rid of it
Forever.
I don't know where
I'll put it.
I guess it'll just stick
In my head
Like glue.

— SAM WINEGARDNER

Finally my "Dad" came "home"
Finally my "Dad" came "home"

From being out of town

For a long time

He came home home yesterday

From going to philedupheia.

And a lot of

Other places

He would come home

and vist

But two days later

He would have to go back.

—BY MEREDITH WEAVER

Finally My "Dad" Came "Home"

Finally my "Dad" came "home"
from being out of town
for a long time.
He came home yesterday
from going to Philadelphia
and a lot of
other places.
He would come home
and visit.
But two days later
he would have to go back.

— MEREDITH WEAVER

Step brothers

I thought my sister and I
were the only children. But on sunday
I found out I have step brothers.
Uh. Oh. More trouble.

Legs

My mom says I have buetiful legs. She
said "Come here legs." I get inberist.
I wish my mom would will stop calling
me legs.

—BY TARONNA BRADFORD

Stepbrothers

I thought my sister and I
were the only children. But on Sunday
I found out I have stepbrothers.
Uh, oh. More trouble.

Legs

My mom says I have beautiful legs. She
says, "Come here, Legs." I get embarrassed.
I wish my mom would stop calling
me "Legs."

— TARONNA BRADFORD

Braces Blues

I hate braces!

They hurt and
People call me names!

Like tin grin and metal mouth,

"When will I get my braces off?"
I ask my mom.../...

I wish I could just float away!

"I hate braces,
    I hate braces,
        I hate braces!"

I hope I get my braces off
SOON!

—BY SARAH C. GABRIEL

Braces Blues

I hate braces!

They hurt and
people call me names

like tin grin and metal mouth.

"When will I get my braces off?"
I ask my mom….

I wish I could just float away

"I hate braces,

I hate braces,

I hate braces!"

I hope I get my braces off
SOON!

— SARAH C. GABRIEL

My best friend
   Is full of ideas
She cheers me up
When I am sad,
We tell secrets to eachother
That are sometimes privet
   I cheer her up,
When she is sad,
      We lern together
We read and right together,
      Someday
We might not be together,
but I'll always remember
Her in my heart.

—BY DARA EMILY SOBISCH

My Best Friend

My best friend
    is full of ideas!
She cheers me up
    when I am sad,
    we tell secrets to each other
    that are sometimes private.
        I cheer her up
when she is sad.
    We learn together,
we read and write together.
    Someday,
we might not be together
but I'll always remember
her in my heart.

—DARA EMILY SOBISCH

Richard

best

Richard is my 1 friend / I don't know why / he ~~cause~~ <ins>calls</ins> me "C" "Coolio," but / I ± like to hang around him anway / He makes me ~~tate~~ <ins>laugh</ins> / He makes silly faces and / pretends to cry when he jumps off the ~~slidxhing~~ <ins>board</ins> ~~bored~~ / We play kickball, / tag / and we eat lunch together / We sit together, on the bus / ~~a~~ during aftercar / and on field trips / I like talking to him / He is my best friend. /

—BY KHALI BALL

Richard

Richard is my best friend.
I don't know why,
he calls me "Coolio," but
I like to hang around with him anyway.
He makes me laugh.
He makes silly faces and
pretends to cry when he jumps off the sliding board.
We play kickball,
tag,
and we eat lunch together.
We sit together on the bus,
during after-care,
and on field trips.
I like talking to him.
He is my best friend.

—KHALI BALL

My Sister

Kayla

Silly
Crazy
abnormal
strange

Who loves

listening to the radio
bugging her sister
sucking up to her parents

Who needs

mental help
a brain transplant
plastic surgery.

Who gives

~~Yucky~~ Kisses
Hugs
Love (occasionally)

Who fears
~~Creepy crawlers~~
Creepy crawlers
Her sister giving her a kiss
Bath time

Who'd like to see

Mickey Mouse
The Hunchback of Notre Dame
Michael Jordan in Person

Teacher of
My God sister Chelsea

Stundent of
Her big sister

Resident of

Planet X

—BY DANIELLE JONES

My Sister Kayla

Silly
Crazy
abnormal
strange

Who loves

listening to the radio
bugging her sister
sucking up to her parents

Who needs

mental help
a brain transplant
plastic surgery

Who gives
Kisses
Hugs
Love (occasionally)

Who fears

Creepy crawlers
Her sister giving her a kiss
Bath time

Who'd like to see

Mickey Mouse
The Hunchback of Notre Dame
Michael Jordan in person

Teacher of
My Godsister Chelsea

Student of
Her big sister

Resident of

Planet X.

—DANIELLE JONES

My Sister Nicole

My sister Nicole,
is always bugging me
and this morning

She yelled at me,
because I told her something
and it was wrong.

She expects me
to let her
see my keyboard.

But my sister Nicole
is still my sister
and I sometimes get

on her nerves too.

—BY LENNEL ECHOLS

My Sister Nicole

My sister Nicole
is always bugging me
and this morning

she yelled at me,
because I told her something,
and it was wrong.

She expects me
to let her
use my keyboard.

But my sister Nicole
is still my sister
and I sometimes get

on her nerves too.

—LENNEL ECHOLS

Claudia

When I grow up/ I want to
be like/ Claudia. (My Mom)

friendly
respectful
consiterite
funny
good cook
good sport
fun to be with

When I grow up/ I want
to be like Claudia.

—BY KELLY MCCORD

72

Claudia

When I grow up
I want to be like
Claudia (My Mom)

friendly
respectful
considerate
funny
good cook
good sport
fun to be with

When I grow up
I want to be like Claudia

—KELLY McCORD

Dream

I had a dream
About my grandpa
We were dancing in his house
In a room with the music on
But it doesn't matter now
Because
A dream is just a dream
And not real

I woke up in the morning
Crying
Knowing he was gone
But the next night
I dreamt agian
Of playing checkers
My granpa's favorite game
But it doesn't matter now
Because
A dream is just a dream
And not real

My mother said
Don't fret
But deep inside my head
I'm dreaming
Dreaming of my grandpa

—BY KATIE
STAMM

Dream

I had a dream
About my grandpa
We were dancing in his house
In a room with the music on
But it doesn't matter now
Because
A dream is just a dream
And not real

I woke up in the morning
Crying
Knowing he was gone
But the next night
I dreamt again
Of playing checkers
My grandpa's favorite game
But it doesn't matter now
Because
A dream is just a dream
And not real

My mother said
Don't fret
But deep inside my head
I'm dreaming

Dreaming of my grandpa

— KATIE STAMM

BAD DAYS

My Mother forgot to
wake me in the morning,

I was late for school

and forgot my homework.
My teacher gave me detention

and everybody laughed.
My friends deserted me

and my little sister
embaressed me.

Oh, I should have stayed

In bed, I said.

—BY REBECCA PURNELL

BAD DAYS

My mother forgot to
wake me in the morning,

I was late for school

and forgot my homework.
My teacher gave me detention

and everybody laughed.
My friends deserted me

and my little sister
embarrassed me.

"Oh, I should have stayed
in bed," I said.

—REBECCA PURNELL

My Dad

"Hi dad" "Hay girl how was school" "It
was o.K" "O.K. Well what did you learn
to, oh boy I'm thinking her he comes
Day) with the questin did anything hapen oh
dad
I go in to my room and cloes the
door
heer some foot seps her he comes

—BY SHERRI TYSINGER

My Dad

"Hi, Dad."
"Hey, girl. How was school?
"It was O.K."
"O.K.? Well, what did you learn today?"
"Oh boy," I'm thinking.
Here he comes
with the question,
"Did anything happen?"
"Oh, Dad."
I go into my room and close the door,
hear some footsteps...
Here he comes.

— SHERRI TYSINGER

Football!

People say "Taylor can't caeth." That's not true. I can caeth only when I'am not under-presher.

—BY TAYLOR JOINER

Football!

People say,
"Taylor can't catch!"
That's not true.
I can catch only
when I'm not under
pressure.

— TAYLOR JOINER

Baseball Stress

Oh no!
I'm up to bat!
I think
What if I get embarressed
Will I hit a grand-slam

The crowd is cheering.
It's the end of the 9th
inning,
What am I going to do?
There's only 38 seconds
left!
Here goes the pitch,
Now I feel persistent,

I hit the ball,
a grand slam!

I run like the wind,
I feel like the road
runner
The outfielders can't

find the ball
e won
13-10 Stars ahead by 3
I did it!
The crowd comes on the
field
Now were off to
a victory party!

— BY TIMOTHY J. COLLINGWOOD

Baseball Stress

Oh, no!
I'm up to bat!
I think,
What if I get embarrassed!
Will I hit a grand slam?

The crowd is cheering,
It's the end of the 9th inning,
What am I going to do?
There's only 30 seconds left!
Here goes the pitch,
Now I feel persistent,

I hit the ball,
A grand slam!

I run like the wind,
I feel like the road runner.

The outfielders can't find the ball.
We won!
13-10, Stars ahead by 3!
I did it!
The crowd comes on the field.
Now we're off to
A victory party!

— TIMOTHY J. COLLINGWOOD

Calarodo River

I am a River
roorring rushing
threw the canon
so steep

I am a River
running thrugh
the south west
so butiatful

I am a River
twisting and turning
thrugh canons
vallys masas and more

I am a River
so blue
so fears

—BY MARYBETH WARGO

84

Colorado River

I am a River
roaring   rushing
through the canyon
so steep

           I am a River
           running   through
           the Southwest
           so beautiful

I am a River
twisting and turning
through   canyons
valleys   mesa   and more

           I am a River
           the Colorado River

— MARYBETH WARGO

Shadows

by Anna Hutt

Shadows
Shadows creeping
In my closet
Under my bed
Shadows watching...
Watching every move I make
Watching....
From behind the bookcase
And in the dusty dresser drawers
Shadows looking
Around the corner
Behind the rocking chair that creeks when it rocks
That creeks when it rocks
Shadows staring
Staring through me
From next to the sofa
And staring through the keyhole in the attic door
Shadows seeing
Seeing everything,
Seeing that I am scared
Seeing that I hurry to get into the sunlight
Shadows following
Following me
Dancing up the walls
Chasing me across the ceiling
Never leaving...
Shadows

— BY ANNA HUTT

Shadows

Shadows
Shadows creeping
In my closet
Under my bed
Shadows watching…
Watching every move I make
Watching...
From behind the bookcase
And in the dusty dresser drawers
Shadows looking
Around the corner
Upon the stairway
Behind the rocking chair that creaks when it rocks
Shadows staring
Staring through me
From next to the sofa
And staring through the keyhole in the attic door
Shadows seeing
Seeing everything
Seeing that I am scared
Seeing that I hurry to get into the sunlight
Shadows following
Following me
Dancing up the walls
Chasing me across the ceiling
Never leaving...
Shadows.

— *ANNA HUTT*

Illustration Credits

Page 39: Stefanie Blejec; *Page 41:* Thomas O'Hagan; *Page 43:* Letisha Jenkins;
Page 45: Maurizio Martinelli; *Page 47:* Lucy McWhorter-Rosen;
Page 49: Artville; *Page 51:* Eleni Bakst; *Page 53:* Odessa Straub;
Page 55: Letisha Jenkins; *Page 57:* Kevin Kocses; *Page 59:* Elli Caroline Marcus;
Page 61: Hannah Ronson and Camilo Burr; *Page 63:* Letisha Jenkins;
Page 65: Elli Caroline Marcus; *Page 67:* Sophia Collas; *Page 69:* Sasha Seckler;
Page 71: Sasha Seckler; *Page 73:* Katie Giberson; *Page 75:* Emma Katz;
Page 77: Christopher Han; *Page 79:* Letisha Jenkins; *Page 81:* Dylan Novelli;
Page 83: Keith Santiago; *Page 85:* Sasha Seroy; *Page 87:* Emily Rose Nagle

Thanks also to:

Roseanne Kurstedt and the students of the New York City Lower Lab School